Kidnapped

ROBERT LOUIS STEVENSON

Level 2

Retold by John Escott
Series Editors: Andy Hopkins and Jocelyn Potter

Pearson Education Limited
Edinburgh Gate, Harlow,
Essex CM20 2JE, England
and Associated Companies throughout the world.

ISBN: 978-1-4058-5537-2

First published by Penguin Books 2000
This edition published 2008

3 5 7 9 10 8 6 4 2

Text copyright © Penguin Books Ltd 2000
This edition copyright © Pearson Education Ltd 2008
Illustrations by David Cuzik (Pennant Illustration)

Typeset by Graphicraft Ltd, Hong Kong
Set in 11/14pt Bembo
Printed in China
SWTC/02

Published by Pearson Education Ltd in association with
Penguin Books Ltd, both companies being subsidiaries of Pearson Plc

For a com ... ite to your local
Pearson ... son Education,
Edinburgh Gate, Harlow, Essex CM20 2JE, England.

Contents

Introduction

There was a sound above my head. I jumped and looked up – at an old gun, at one of the windows.

'I – I'm here with a letter,' I said. 'A letter for Mr Ebenezer Balfour of Shaws. Is he here?'

'Put it down outside the door, and go away,' said the man with the gun.

After his parents die, young David Balfour starts his journey to the strange House of Shaws. He is going to live with his uncle. But people look strangely at him when he talks about the place. 'Stay away from there. Stay away!' a man on the road tells him.

Ebenezer Balfour is an old man, but he is dangerous. He puts David on a ship to America, and a difficult time begins. Can the man in expensive French clothes help David? Or is life more dangerous with him than without him?

At the time of this story, King George was the king of England, Scotland and Ireland, but there were a lot of unhappy people in Scotland and Ireland. They wanted another Catholic king from the Stuart family (Stewart in this story). They fought the king's soldiers, but they lost. After the fight at Culloden, in 1746, Charles Edward Stuart had to leave Scotland. This story begins five years later.

Robert Louis Stevenson was born in Edinburgh in Scotland in 1850. He was a weak child and he was ill for most of his life. He went on long journeys and in 1888 he moved to Samoa, a warm country, with his American wife. He died there in 1894. His most famous books are *Treasure Island*, *The Strange Case of Dr Jekyll and Mr Hyde* and *Kidnapped*. They are all Penguin Readers.

Chapter 1   The House of Shaws

Early one morning in June 1751 I left my father's house in Essendean for the last time. I walked down the road, and met that good man Mr Campbell near his church.

'Did you have some breakfast, David Balfour, my boy?' he asked.

'Yes, Mr Campbell. Thank you,' I answered.

'Then I'll walk with you to the river,' he said.

We walked quietly for a time. Then Mr Campbell said, 'Now, Davie, I've got something for you. It's a letter from your father. He gave it to me after your mother died. Before *he* died. He said, "Give it to David after they sell the house. Then he has to take it to the house of Shaws, near Cramond. Please tell him that." Here's the letter, David.'

'The house of Shaws?' I said. 'Why did he want me to go there?'

'I don't know,' said Mr Campbell. 'I think your father came from there. It's the home of the family Balfour of Shaws. Perhaps your father came from that family. He never spoke about it. He was a clever man. Cleverer than most village school teachers.'

Mr Campbell put the letter into my hand, and I read on it: 'To Ebenezer Balfour of Shaws. My son, David Balfour, will give this letter to him.'

I was seventeen years old, and the son of a country teacher. I planned to go to Edinburgh. I wanted to be a student in one of the great schools there.

'Mr Campbell,' I said, 'do I have to go?'

'Cramond isn't a long way from Edinburgh,' he answered. 'You can walk there in two days.'

At the river, Mr Campbell took my hand in his hands. He

1

suddenly looked very sad. 'Goodbye, Davie,' he said. And he turned and went quickly away.

I carried my little bag across the river, then started to climb the hill. At the top, I turned and looked back at Essendean village for the last time.

◆

Two days later, in the morning, I came to the top of a hill. I could see the city of Edinburgh, and ships on the sea.

I started to walk down the hill. After a time I saw a man, and I asked him the way to Cramond. 'It's to the west of the city,' he said. On my way down, I asked two or three more people. Then I came to the Edinburgh to Glasgow road.

When I was near Cramond, I began to ask the way to the house of Shaws. People looked at me strangely. 'Is it because of my clothes?' I thought. 'I'm a country boy and I'm going to a great house. Do they think that's strange? Or is there something strange about the *house*?'

I changed my question when I spoke to the next man.

'Do you know the house of Shaws?' I asked.

'Yes,' he said. 'Why?'

'Is it a big house?' I asked.

'Oh yes. It's big,' he said.

'And the people in it?' I said.

'People?' he said. 'What's wrong with you? There aren't any people.'

'Oh!' I said. 'Not Mr Ebenezer?'

'Oh yes,' he said. '*He's* there. What do you want from him?'

'Perhaps I can get work,' I said.

'What!' He moved nearer me. 'Listen!' he said. 'Stay away from there. Stay away!'

◆

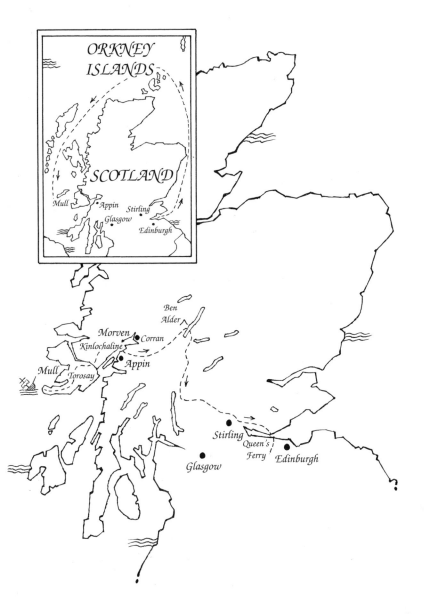

It was nearly dark when I found the house. I stood and looked at it. 'I don't like it,' I thought. 'There are walls, but no glass in the windows!' I could see the light of a little fire in one of the rooms. I went to the thick, heavy door and hit it.

No answer. Everything was quiet.

'Is somebody listening to me in there?' I thought. I could hear a clock when I put my ear to the door. I nearly ran away, but suddenly I was angry. I kicked the door and shouted for Mr Balfour.

There was a sound above my head. I jumped and looked up – at an old gun, at one of the windows.

'I – I'm here with a letter,' I said. 'A letter for Mr Ebenezer Balfour of Shaws. Is he here?'

'Put it down outside the door, and go away,' said the man with the gun.

'I will not!' I said, angrily. 'I'll put it into Mr Balfour's hand. It's a letter about me.'

'And who are you?' was the next question.

'My name is David Balfour,' I said.

The man was quiet for a minute. Then he said, 'Is your father dead? Yes, of course he's dead – you're here.' He stopped and thought. 'Wait there and I'll come down.'

Chapter 2   My Uncle

After a time, somebody turned a key in the door. Then the door opened a little. I moved inside – and it shut quickly after me.

'Go into the kitchen,' said the man.

And he turned the key in the door again.

I found the kitchen. There was light from a small fire, but no other light. There was a table, with a plate of food and a drink on it. It was a big room, and there were large boxes near one wall.

A small, grey man came into the kitchen. He was about sixty years old. He watched me but never looked at my face.

'Who is he?' I thought. 'What is his work here?'

'Are you hungry?' he asked. 'You can have that food.'

'But it's your dinner,' I said.

'That's all right,' he said. 'I'll have the drink.' He drank, then put out his hand. 'Give me the letter.'

'The letter isn't for you,' I said. 'It's for Mr Balfour.'

'And who do you think I am?' he said. 'Give me Alexander's letter.'

'You know my father's name?' I said.

'Of course,' he said. 'He was my brother. I'm your uncle, Davie. So give me the letter. Then sit down and eat.'

I gave him the letter, then ate some food.

'So your father is dead,' he said suddenly. 'Did he tell you anything about me?'

'No,' I said. 'He never said anything about a brother.'

'Ah!' he said. 'And did he say anything about Shaws?'

'I never heard the name,' I said.

'That's strange,' he said. But he smiled. 'Now it's time for bed. I'll show you the way.'

He took me up some stairs without a light. Then he opened a door. The room inside was dark too.

'I want a light,' I told him.

'No lights in this house,' he said. 'I'm afraid of fire. Good night.' And he pushed me into the room.

Then he turned the key in the door.

The room was cold. And the bed – when I found it – was not dry. That night, I slept on the floor.

◆

The next morning, breakfast was small. In the room next to the kitchen I found a lot of books. Inside one of them were some

'Give me the letter.'

words in my father's writing: *To my younger brother Ebenezer on his birthday*.

I couldn't understand it. The writing was my father's, but it was not the writing of a child. So Ebenezer was the *younger* brother. Then why did he have the family house? Before my father died, he had very little money. What did it mean?

I looked at the books, then cleaned the room. It was a hot day, and I thought, 'There'll be rain and lightning later.'

That evening at dinner, my uncle spoke very kindly to me.

'You can help me with the house and garden, Davie,' he said. 'And I'll help you. But I'll want some papers before I can do that. They're in a box at the top of the stairs at the other end of the house. You can only get to the stairs from the outside. Here's the key.' And he pulled a big old key out of his coat. 'Go in, and up the stairs, and bring down the box.'

I asked, 'Can I have a light, sir?'

'No,' he said. 'No lights in this house.'

He opened the big door, and I went out into the night. I put my hands on the walls and found my way to the door at the end. The key turned in the door, but not easily. Then I found the stairs inside. I started to climb – higher and higher.

I climbed about 120 feet, then the rain began. Suddenly, lightning moved quickly across the sky. And I saw something! I stopped and cried out! *There were no more stairs*! And it was a long way down! Then everything was dark again.

'My uncle sent me up here ...' I thought. 'He ... *wants to kill me!*'

◆

I came down the stairs very carefully. Sometimes lightning lit the stairs, but most of the time it was dark. And dangerous.

I came out of the door. Suddenly, lightning showed me my uncle at the other door. He didn't see me. He was afraid of the lightning, and he ran into the house.

When I walked into the kitchen, his face went white.

'You – you're all right?' he said.

'Yes, thank you!' I said angrily.

I wanted to ask questions but he said, 'I'll tell you about it in the morning. I want to go to bed now. I'm ill – very ill.'

I shut him in his room and turned the key in his door. Then I went back to the kitchen and made a big fire. That night I slept on the boxes.

Chapter 3 The Ship

Next morning, I opened the door of my uncle's room. But before he could tell me anything, we heard somebody at the door.

I opened it and found a boy outside. 'I'm here with a letter,' he said. 'And I'm very hungry.'

'Come into the house,' I said. 'I'll give you some food.'

When the boy started eating, my uncle read the letter. Then he gave it to me. It said:

Sir,

I am now at the Hawes Hotel, and my ship is ready for sea. Do you want to speak to me again? Tell me today.

I talked to your lawyer, Mr Rankeillor. Perhaps we will lose money because of this.

Elias Hoseason

After I read it, my uncle said, 'Hoseason is the captain of a ship, the *Covenant*. You and I can go with this boy and see the captain at the Hawes Hotel. I will put my name to some papers. Then we can visit Mr Rankeillor, the lawyer. He knew your father.'

8

So we went. My uncle never said a word all the way. But the boy talked. His name was Ransome.

'I first went to sea when I was nine,' he told me.

I asked him about the *Covenant*. 'There isn't a finer ship on the sea,' he said. And about Captain Hoseason, he said, 'He's a fine captain. He isn't afraid of anything or anybody. But he isn't a seaman. Mr Shuan, the first officer, is. He can take the ship anywhere in the world. The other people really do have a bad time.'

He talked more. These 'other people', I understood, were murderers and other bad men on their way to work in North America. Then there were children – kidnapped children. The captain sold them when the ship arrived in America.

At the Hawes Hotel, my uncle went in to see Captain Hoseason. They began a long talk with a lot of papers.

◆

I went across the road and down to the sea. The ship's boat was there and some men from the *Covenant* stood near it. Then a man from the hotel came and spoke to me.

'Did you come with Ebenezer?' he asked. 'When I look at you, I remember Mr Alexander. He was a good man.'

'Isn't Ebenezer good?' I asked.

'No,' said the man from the hotel. 'He *was* a fine young man. But he's a bad old man now.'

I saw Captain Hoseason go down to the ship's boat and speak to the men. He was a tall man and not the hard man of Ransome's stories. Then he came across to me.

'Sir,' he said, 'Mr Balfour spoke about you. You're a fine young man. Come to my ship with your uncle. We'll have a drink.'

I wanted to see the inside of the ship. But was it dangerous?

'My uncle and I have to see a lawyer this afternoon,' I said.

9

'He told me about that,' said the captain. 'But we'll go very near the town. The ship's boat can take you there later. You'll be very near Rankeillor's place.' And when my uncle came to us, the captain suddenly spoke very quietly in my ear. 'Be careful of the old man,' he said. 'He's planning something bad for you. Come on to the ship. I'll tell you about it.'

So I got into the boat with him. My uncle got in and sat next to me. When we arrived at the ship, the captain climbed quickly up. Then he called me and I followed him. He showed me the interesting things on the ship.

'Where is my uncle?' I said suddenly.

'That's a good question,' said Hoseason. He was not friendly now.

I was suddenly afraid. I ran and looked at the sea. Yes! There was the ship's boat! It was nearly at the town again! And my uncle was in it!

I cried, 'Help! Help!'

My uncle turned round. His face was hard and cold ... and afraid.

Then strong hands pulled me away. There was a CRASH! I saw a great light – and then everything went black.

Chapter 4   To Sea

I woke up. It was dark, but I could hear the sounds of a ship in strong winds. And then I knew. I was somewhere near the bottom of a ship, and we were at sea.

I hated my uncle! He was a bad, dangerous man – I knew that now.

'I was stupid!' I thought. 'What is going to happen to me now?'

After some time, I fell asleep.

◆

A light woke me. A small man with green eyes looked down at me. 'How are you?' he said.

I couldn't answer. The back of my head hurt, and he looked at it. Then he began to wash it.

'It'll hurt for a long time,' he said. 'Did you have any food?'

'I can't eat anything,' I said.

He gave me a drink from a cup, and then went away.

When the man came again, the captain came with him.

'Why did you bring me here, Mr Riach?' the captain asked.

'You can see, sir,' said Riach. 'He's very ill. He can't eat. And there's no light in here. We've got to put him in the seamen's room.'

'He will stay here,' said the captain. He turned away.

Riach put a hand on his arm and said, 'I'm the second officer on this old ship. Nobody pays me to murder–'

'What!' shouted Hoseason. 'You know me! I'm a hard man, but I'm not a murderer. Are you saying the boy will die?'

'Yes, he will,' said Riach.

'All right,' said Hoseason. 'Move him.'

Five minutes later, a man carried me up to the seamen's room. There they put me down on a small bed. Then I knew nothing for hours – or days.

◆

The men tried to be kind to me. They gave me back my money – most of it.

'You'll want it,' they said. 'The ship is going to the Carolinas.'

At that time – when I was young – people sold men for work. Black men and white men. That was my uncle's plan for me.

The ship's boy, Ransome, came in from the roundhouse sometimes. Mr Shuan, the first officer, often hit him and hurt

11

him badly. But to the men, Shuan was a fine man. 'The only good seaman on the ship,' they said. 'And not a bad man when he isn't drinking.'

◆

Day after day and night after night the ship fought its way north in strong winds. I got better and stronger, but I could not leave the room.

One night, at about twelve o'clock, a seaman came down for his coat. After some time, the men there began talking.

'Shuan hit him too hard this time,' they said.

Who did Shuan hit? We all knew. We did not have to ask the name. Suddenly, Captain Hoseason came into the room. He looked round, and came to me.

He spoke quite kindly. 'We want you to work in the roundhouse,' he said. 'Go now.'

I ran up from the seamen's room. The strong sea came up across the ship and nearly pushed me into the water. Then a kind seaman helped me. He showed me the roundhouse.

On my way there I went past two other seamen. They carried Ransome down to my old room.

Chapter 5   The Roundhouse

The roundhouse wasn't round. It was square. (It was the 'roundhouse' because you could walk round it.) It had a table and two small beds. There was a room under the roundhouse. Here were the best food and drink, and the small guns. There were one or two seamen's swords, but most of the swords were outside.

When I arrived, Mr Shuan sat at the table with a bottle in front of him. Captain Hoseason came in. He stood and looked at Shuan. He said nothing. After a time, Mr Riach came in.

'The boy's dead,' he told the captain.

Mr Shuan said nothing. He put out his hand to the bottle. Mr Riach quickly took the bottle away. Shuan jumped up. He wanted to kill Riach, but the captain stopped him.

'Shuan!' Hoseason shouted. 'You murdered the boy!'

Shuan put his head in his hands. 'He brought me a dirty cup,' he said.

Hoseason took him to his bed. 'Go to sleep,' he said quietly.

The murderer cried a little, then he fell asleep.

◆

I had to bring the food to the captain and the first and second officers. And I had to take them a drink when they wanted one. My bed was on the floor of the roundhouse.

For ten more days the *Covenant* fought her way north and then west in strong winds. Then the captain turned south and looked for a way round the south of Ireland. The wind got weaker after a time. Then there was heavy rain, and we could not see anything.

It was about ten o'clock at night when the ship hit something. The captain and Mr Riach were in the roundhouse. The two men jumped up.

'We hit a boat!' said Hoseason.

The captain was right. And the other boat broke and went down to the bottom of the sea. Only one man on it did not die. The other men went down with the boat.

We got the man on to our ship. Then Hoseason brought him into the roundhouse. He was a small man, but strong. His face was dark from the sun, and he smiled a lot. When he took off his coat, he put two very fine guns on the table. And he had a long sword.

The captain looked at the man's clothes. They were very fine clothes for the roundhouse of the *Covenant*.

13

'A beautiful French coat,' said Hoseason.

'Oh!' said the man. 'You mean—' And he put his hands quickly on his guns.

'Wait!' said the captain.

'Oh,' said the man. 'Are you one of us?'

'Am I fighting the king's soldiers?' said Hoseason. 'No. But you have problems because you are. That isn't right, and I'm sorry about that.'

'Are you really?' asked the man. 'I don't want to get into the hands of the soldiers with red coats. Now, sir, I am trying to get to France. There was a French ship near here, but we didn't see it in the dark and the rain. I have some money. It is my chieftain's, but I can use some of it. Will you take me to France, captain?'

'I can't do that,' said Hoseason. 'But perhaps I can put you on land near here. I want to see the money first, of course.'

He sent me away — I had to get food for the man. I was very quick. When I came back, the stranger paid sixty pounds out of a heavy money bag. Hoseason said, 'I'll take you to the Linnhe Loch★ for your sixty pounds.' Then he left the roundhouse.

I knew about the people of the Highlands†. They paid the king or the chieftain for the use of their land. But many of the Highlanders' chieftains lived in France. Good men, I knew, took the money from the clans to the chieftains. And here was one of them.

I put the food in front of him.

'Bring me a bottle,' he said. 'I want a drink for my sixty pounds.'

I went out for the captain's key. I saw him with the two officers. Mr Riach said, 'Can't we move him out of the roundhouse?'

★ Loch: a name, in Scotland, for water with land round it.
† Highlands: the mountains of Scotland. The people there are Highlanders.

'He's better there,' answered Hoseason. 'He can't use his sword in there.'

I wanted to turn away from these murderers. But I said, 'Captain, the man wants a drink. Can I have the key?'

They all turned round.

'He can get the guns!' said Riach. And then to me: 'Can you find the guns, David?'

'Yes, David can bring them to us,' said Hoseason. 'He's a good boy. David, that Highlander is dangerous, and no friend of King George. You'll help us – Yes? We'll give you some of the man's money.'

They told me their plan. Then they sent me with the keys to the drinks and gun room.

♦

The man looked up from his food when I went into the roundhouse. I put my hand on his arm and said, 'Do you want them to kill you?'

He stood up quickly. 'What do you mean?' he asked.

'They're all murderers on this ship,' I said. 'They murdered a boy. Now it's you.'

'Will you help me?' he asked.

'Yes,' I said. 'I'm not a murderer.'

'Good,' he said. 'What's your name?'

'David Balfour,' I said. 'David Balfour of Shaws.'

'My name is Stewart – a king's name,' he said. 'But they call me Alan Breck.'

We looked at the roundhouse. I shut one of the strong doors. Before I shut the other door, he said, 'No, David. When the door is open, most of the men will be in front of me. And I want them to be in front of me when we fight.' Then he asked me about the guns. 'How many are there?'

'Fifteen,' I said.

'Oh!' said Alan. He was quiet for a minute. Then he said, 'I'll be at this door. You watch the other door. When the guns are ready, stand on that bed near the window. Be ready for them.'

I was afraid. But I did it.

Chapter 6   The Fight

The men outside waited for me, but then the captain came to the open door.

'Stop!' said Alan. He had his sword in his hand.

The captain said nothing. He turned and looked at me with an angry face. Then he went away.

It came suddenly. There was a shout, and then Mr Shuan was at the door. He fought Alan.

'Watch your window!' said Alan. And before I turned, his sword went through the first officer's stomach.

I looked quickly through my window. Five men ran to the other door with some heavy wood. I started shooting at them with my first gun. One of them shouted when I hit him. I shot again, but it went over their heads. But they threw down the wood and ran away.

I couldn't see across the room because of the smoke from my gun. Alan was all right, but Mr Shuan was on the floor.

'They'll be back, David,' Alan said. 'Watch from your window.'

I got my guns ready again. Then I waited.

Suddenly some men with swords ran to the open door. Then the window above my head broke and a man jumped through. His sword fell from his hand. Before he could take it again, I put a gun to his back.

But I couldn't shoot. He turned quickly, and put his hands on me. Then I was really afraid, so I shot him in the stomach. He fell to the floor.

16

Then the leg of a second man hit me on the head. I looked up when he came through the window. I quickly took another gun and shot him in the leg.

'David!' shouted Alan. A seaman had his arms round Alan.

I took the sword of a dead man and ran to Alan. But before I could do anything, Alan jumped away from the man. He shouted and used his sword fast and angrily. The seaman and his friends turned and ran.

There were four dead men inside the roundhouse. Alan and I threw them outside.

Nothing happened for a long time. One of us sat at the door and watched. The other slept.

At about six o'clock in the morning we sat down and had breakfast. Alan ate fast, but I was not very hungry. This was my first fight.

Alan cut a shiny button from his coat. 'My father, Duncan Stewart, gave me these buttons,' he said. 'Now I'm giving you one so you will remember last night's work. Show the button anywhere, and Alan Breck's friends will be your friends.'

Mr Riach called from outside. The captain wanted to talk to Alan.

'What will he do?' I said.

'He won't try anything,' Riach answered. 'He can't. The men won't help him. And I'm afraid, Davie. We want to see the man off this ship. We'll take him to Linnhe Loch.'

Chapter 7   The 'Red Fox'

The nearest way to Linnhe Loch was to the north of the island of Mull. But the captain didn't know that way. So we went down the west of Mull, and came round the south of the island.

Alan and I sat and told our stories. First I told him my story.

17

'Show the button anywhere, and Alan Breck's friends
will be your friends.'

He listened kindly. But he was angry when I spoke about that good friend of mine in Essendean, Mr Campbell. Then he shouted, 'I hate everybody with that name!'

'Why?' I asked. 'Mr Campbell's a good man. What's wrong with the Campbells?'

'I'm a Stewart from Appin,' said Alan. 'The Campbells hate us. They want our lands and houses, and they try everything. They use lawyers – but never a sword. The Campbells make life dangerous for me and my friends.'

'But you are going home?' I said.

'Oh yes!' said Alan. 'I come home every year. I have to see my friends and my country. France is a fine place, of course, but I have to see Scotland. And then there's my chieftain, Ardshiel. All his life he was a great man, David. He had a king's name, and 400 swordsmen. And now he has to live in a French town. Now, the people of Appin have to pay King George of England so they can use their land. But they love their chieftain, and they find money for Ardshiel too. So, David, I carry that money.' And he hit the money bag hard with his hand. 'Ardshiel's brother, James Stewart, gets it from people. I carry it.'

I thought about the clansmen's love of their chieftain. 'I understand,' I said. 'I'm not fighting the king's men, but I understand.'

'Yes,' he said. 'You're a good man and you understand. But the Campbells don't. And the Red Fox–' He stopped, and there was hate in his eyes.

'The Red Fox?' I said. 'Who is he?'

'I'll tell you,' said Alan. 'Ardshiel had to run with his wife and their children after the fight with the English at Culloden. It was difficult, but they got to France. And the English took away all Ardshiel's land; they took the swords and guns from his clansmen. But they could not kill the clansmen's love for their chieftain.'

'The money in your bag shows that,' I said.

'Yes,' said Alan. 'But there is a man with red hair, a Campbell – Colin of Glenure–'

'The Red Fox?' I said.

'Yes,' said Alan. 'He got papers from King George. The papers made him the king's man in the lands of Appin. The clansmen had to pay him for their land. But of course they sent money to Ardshiel too. He was very angry about that. He sent for lawyers and papers and soldiers. He sent all Ardshiel's people away from their homes and their lands. The soldiers are there now. Hundreds of them. But the money gets through to Ardshiel. The soldiers can't stop it.'

'But I don't understand,' I said. 'There are soldiers in the Highlands. But they don't catch you. How do you do it?'

'It's not difficult,' said Alan. 'A soldier is in one place, so you go a different way. And everywhere you find friends. "Where are the soldiers?" you ask them. And they tell you. They are good people, and you can stay in their houses. They give you food, and a bed for the night. And the soldiers don't watch very well because the clansmen have no guns or swords.' He smiled. 'Or they think that. But there *are* some, under floors and in other places. The soldiers don't know about them.'

Chapter 8   In the Water

We got nearer to the island of Mull, and now there were more and more rocks in the sea. The sea began to move more quickly. The captain sent a man high up on the ship. Suddenly, this man called, 'Rocks! Stay away from the land!'

But then the wind changed. The sea turned the ship – right on to the rocks! There was a CRASH!

Mr Riach and some seamen ran to the ship's boat. It was in

the middle of the ship. I ran and helped them.

Suddenly somebody shouted something, and the sea threw the ship right, then left. The sea came over the ship. It pulled me out of the ship and into the water!

I went down in the water and fought my way up again, many times. And the sea pushed me away from the ship.

After a time I found some wood from the ship and put my hands round it. Then, suddenly, I was in quieter water. I looked for the ship. It was a long way away. I could see it, but I couldn't see the boat in the water.

I saw land. I am not a good swimmer. But I stayed with the wood and kicked with my legs. After about an hour, I could put my feet on the bottom and walk to the land.

I was wet, very tired, cold and hungry. I started to walk away from the sea. I wanted to find a house. 'In a house I can get dry and warm,' I thought. 'And they can tell me about the ship and the men on it.'

It was difficult ground. I walked across the rocks and came to more water. There was land across the water. I turned and climbed over more rocks. But after a time, I understood. I was on a small island, with no houses and no people. The big island of Mull was across the water.

I walked across the small island again and looked for my wood. I carried it across the island and then put it into the water at the nearest place to Mull. I swam across with it. When I climbed up the rocks on Mull, some money fell from my coat. Most of my money was with the seamen at the bottom of the sea! I left Essendean with more than fifty pounds. Now I only had about three pounds.

I went down in the water and fought my way up again . . .

Chapter 9   The Shiny Button

I was tired, wet, weak and cold, so I found a place between two rocks. I think I slept. The sun woke me, and I found a very small river. I drank, and then I went to sleep again in the sun, next to the river. It was afternoon when I climbed a hill. I looked at the country from the top.

There was smoke to the north-east – smoke from a house. I was very tired, but I started walking to it.

I arrived at the house at about six o'clock in the evening. It was long and low. An old man sat outside in the evening sun. He didn't speak English well. But I understood a little. The men from the ship were on the island.

'Was there one man in expensive clothes?' I asked.

'Yes,' he said. 'Oh! You're the boy with the shiny button!'

'Yes,' I said. And I showed him the button.

'He will meet you in his country,' said the man. 'He told me that. Go through Torosay.' And he took me into his little house.

His wife could speak no English. She smiled and put their best food in front of me. The old man made a wonderful drink. After that, I slept well. It was nearly twelve o'clock when I woke up next day. Then the old woman made me breakfast.

I tried to pay them, but they didn't want any money.

The old man came to the door with me.

'That's the way to Torosay,' he said. 'There are no roads. You'll have to ask.'

I did ask. There were many people at work on the hills, and with their animals. Their clothes were strange. They could not wear their Highland clothes. Highland clothes showed a man's clan, and the English king wanted to end the clans.

Not many people could speak English. I said, 'Torosay?', but they did not show me the way. They spoke words, but I could not understand the language. So my journey was slow and long.

There is a boat every day from Torosay to Kinlochaline. Torosay and Kinlochaline are in the country of the Maclean clan. But Neil Roy Macrob took me on the boat. Macrob was one of the names of Alan's clansmen, so I wanted to talk to Neil Roy. But I couldn't do it with other people in the boat.

At Kinlochaline, I talked to him. 'You're one of the Appin men?' I said.

'Yes,' he answered. 'Why?'

I said, 'I'm looking for somebody. His name is Alan Breck Stewart.'

He was suddenly not very friendly. 'He's in France,' he said.

I showed him the button.

'Why didn't you show me that first?' he said. 'You're the boy with the button. I have to help you on your way. Stay in Kinlochaline tonight. Then tomorrow you can go across Morven to Corran on the Linnhe Loch. You'll find my brother Alec there, and he'll take you to another place in his boat.'

I said, 'Thank you.'

'Listen to me,' he said. 'Never say the name of Alan Breck. And don't speak to anybody on the way. Stay away from Campbells and the red soldiers. When you see soldiers, leave the road. Go behind a tree.'

Chapter 10   The End of Red Fox

Neil Roy Macrob's brother took me in his boat to a place in Alan's country of Appin. I got out of the boat somewhere near the trees. Behind and above the trees I could see high mountains.

There was a small road. I sat down near it and looked round. After a time, I heard men and horses. Two men came along the road. The first man was big with red hair. He was very hot and red in the face. The second man was in black clothes. 'A lawyer,' I

24

thought. They stopped when they saw me. There were other men behind them.

'What are you doing here?' asked the man with red hair.

'I'm looking for James of Aucharn,' I said.

'James of Aucharn?' he said. He turned to the lawyer. 'Is he going to fight, do you think?'

'I don't know, Glenure,' said the lawyer. 'But I'll say this again. Why don't we wait here for the soldiers?'

I knew then. The man with red hair was Colin of Glenure – the Red Fox.

'You don't have to be afraid of me,' I said, 'I'm not one of James Stewart's men, and I'm not one of yours. I'm nobody's man, only King George's.'

'Good boy!' said Glenure. 'But I am an important man here, and–'

Suddenly, there was the sound of a gun from somewhere up on the hill. At the same time, Glenure fell down on the road.

'I'm dying!' he said. 'Be careful! I'm dying.'

The lawyer went down and took Glenure in his arms. But he could do nothing for the man with red hair.

For a minute I did nothing. Then I shouted, 'The murderer!' I started to run through the trees and up the hill behind them.

When I came to the top, I saw the murderer. He was a big man in a black coat. He had a long gun.

'Here!' I shouted down to the men on the road. 'I can see him!'

The murderer looked round. Then he ran through some trees and out on to the mountain above them. I followed quickly. I was near the higher trees when somebody cried, 'Stop!'

I looked round. The lawyer shouted, 'Come down!' to me. Soldiers with red coats started to come through the trees below me. They carried guns, and they climbed fast.

'Come down, boy!' shouted the lawyer.

'No!' I called down to him. 'You come up! We can catch him.'

'I'll give you ten pounds when you take that boy!' the lawyer called to the soldiers. 'He's with them! They sent him here and he stopped Glenure. Get him! Kill him!'

He shouted to the soldiers, but I heard him. I suddenly understood. 'They think I'm working with the murderer!' I thought.

Some of the soldiers began to move up to me. Other soldiers put up their guns. I couldn't move.

'Quickly!' said somebody near me. 'In here! In the trees!'

I ran into the trees. Then I heard the guns.

Alan Breck stood under the trees. He said, 'Come with me!' and started running. I followed him.

We ran through the trees and round rocks on the mountain. We ran fast. I couldn't think and I couldn't speak. But sometimes Alan stood and looked at the soldiers. Then I understood. He wanted the soldiers to see him! Every time, we heard excited shouts from the soldiers behind us.

After quarter of an hour, Alan stopped. He sat down on the ground and turned to me.

'Now,' he said, 'this is important. Follow me – for your life!'

We moved fast, but more carefully. We turned and ran back across the hill. Then Alan suddenly sat down under the trees. I fell down next to him.

Chapter 11   James Stewart

Alan got up first. He looked out from the trees.

'The soldiers are going away,' he said, when he came back to me.

'Alan,' I said, 'we have to go different ways.'

'Why?' he said.

'That Campbell man is dead in the road,' I said. 'It was murder, and I don't want– '

'Murder!' cried Alan. 'Listen, Mr Balfour of Shaws. When I want to kill a man, I won't do it in my country. It makes things difficult for my clan. I didn't kill him.'

I was very happy about that.

'But they'll look for us for the murder,' he said. 'And you'll have to stay with me because you don't know the country.'

'I don't have to run away,' I said. 'I'm not afraid of the law. I didn't do anything wrong. But I want to go to Stirling. I want to talk to my uncle's lawyer. He has some papers for me.'

'You're in the Highlands,' he said. 'The "law" here is the law of the Campbells. The dead man is a Campbell. So somebody will have to die for his murder. And you, Mr Balfour of Shaws, will be the right person.'

'Oh,' I said.

'We'll have to run,' said Alan. 'It will be hard in the sun and rain and wind. But I'm not going to die. And I will take you to Stirling.'

◆

We walked over the hills and mountains. Sometimes we had to move on our stomachs. Then it was dark. After a time, we saw a light.

'That's James's house,' said Alan. 'It's late for a light. Something's wrong.'

He was right. James Stewart knew about the murder.

Men and women moved quickly. 'The soldiers are coming,' they said. They took guns and swords from under the floor of the house. They carried them outside and put them into the ground. James's wife looked at a large number of papers and put some of them into the fire.

27

'It's dangerous for you here,' James said to Alan. 'You can leave Ardshiel's money. My son will take it tonight. You two have to go away now – and fast! A long way away.'

One of James's sons gave me some clothes and some good Highland shoes. He gave me a sword and guns and food.

Alan and I ate quickly, and then James Stewart said, 'Now go. It will be light in an hour or two, and the soldiers will come.'

◆

Sometimes we walked; sometimes we ran. When it was light, we ran faster. We were between the mountains, but there were not many trees.

'That rock!' said Alan. 'Over there!' The big rock was about half a mile away. 'We'll have to run.'

We ran to it. I was very tired and I nearly fell. I call it 'a rock', but it was really two big rocks.

'Help me up,' said Alan. And I pushed him on top of the rocks. Then he put his coat down and pulled me up.

It was a good place. We could sleep between the tops of the two rocks. Nobody on the ground could see us.

'I was stupid,' said Alan suddenly. 'First I took the wrong road, so we are in a really bad place. And worse, we're going to be here on a long hot summer day without a water-bottle.'

Chapter 12   Alan Breck, Murderer

At about nine in the morning, I woke up. Alan's hand was across my mouth. 'Don't speak!' he said very quietly. 'You talked in your sleep.'

'Oh?' I said. 'But why did you wake me?'

He looked over the rock with one eye, and I did the same. It was a sunny day and the sky was blue. A river ran between the mountains. Less than half a mile up the river there were a lot of soldiers. They stood and sat round a fire. Near them there was another rock. It was as high as ours. On the top was a man with a gun. There were more soldiers next to the river. Some were on horses.

Alan said, very quietly, 'They're watching the river. We're all right up here, but we don't want them to come up the hill. They'll see us. There are not many of them at the widest place on the river. So when night comes, we'll try to get past them there.'

'And what are we going to do all day?' I asked.

'We stay here and the sun will cook us,' he said.

The rock got hotter and hotter. At about two o'clock we couldn't stay there. There was now a place out of the sun at the back of the rock.

'We have to move,' said Alan. He jumped down to the ground, and I followed him. We sat out of the sun for an hour or two. We were very weak and very thirsty. No soldier came or saw us.

Out of the sun, we felt a little stronger. So we began to move, very carefully. We went from rock to rock across the hill. I followed Alan. Sometimes we went on our stomachs, sometimes we had to run.

When the sun started to go down, we came to a small river. It ran down into the bigger river. It was wonderful. We drank, and we put our heads under the cold water. We stayed there and waited for night.

When night came, we moved again. We were very careful. Then we went very fast, and left the soldiers behind us.

◆

For three days, we walked at night and slept in the day. We only spoke to one man. Alan knew him. He showed us a paper, and we read about the murderer of Colin of Glenure. 'Alan Breck, the murderer,' it said, 'wore a blue French coat, with shiny buttons . . .'

We went from rock to rock across the hill.

My name wasn't there, because nobody knew my name. I was 'his helper: a tall strong boy of about eighteen in an old blue coat . . .' (and my clothes and shoes before I got other clothes from James's son).

After four days, we were very tired. We could not see anybody below us. So we came down from the mountains and on to the open ground below. At about twelve o'clock, we were near the middle of the open ground. We stopped.

'You sleep first,' said Alan.

I was tired when he woke me. Alan went to sleep and I began to watch. Perhaps it was the hot sun, but I slept again.

I woke up and looked round me.

Soldiers!

I saw them on their horses and woke Alan. He looked at the soldiers, and then at me. He didn't say, 'You were asleep,' but he knew it.

'Do you see that mountain?' he said. 'It's Ben Alder. There are a lot of good places up there. Let's go.'

He started to move across the ground on his stomach, very quickly. I followed him. We did it for hour after hour.

When it started to get dark, I said, 'I'm nearly dead. Can't we stop?'

'No,' said Alan. 'Before day comes, you and I have to find a place on Ben Alder.'

Chapter 13   The Lawyer

We saw other soldiers after that, but they were not dangerously near us. Then we arrived at the River Forth in Stirling. There were a lot of soldiers there, and we couldn't use the bridge over the river.

'We'll have to get a boat,' said Alan.

31

We walked through a village, and Alan said, 'Did you see the pretty girl in the bread shop?'

'Yes,' I said. 'A very pretty girl.'

'Right,' he said. 'She'll look at you and think, "He's tired and ill." Now, listen . . .'

And he told me his plan.

We went into the little shop. Alan nearly carried me. He put me in a chair and gave me some bread and water.

'He's very ill,' he told the girl. 'I have to take him across the river to the doctor.'

She took us across the river in her father's boat, but she did not tell her father.

◆

I was in the street early. I wanted to find Mr Rankeillor, the lawyer. 'Will he look at my dirty clothes and send me away?' I thought. 'What can I do?'

I stood outside a fine house and made a plan. Alan was in the trees outside the town.

A man came out of the house. He looked at me.

'What are you doing?' he asked.

'I'm looking for Mr Rankeillor,' I said.

'I am Mr Rankeillor,' he said. 'But I don't know your name, or your face.'

'My name is David Balfour,' I said.

His eyes opened wide. 'Where did you come from, Mr Balfour?' he said.

'From many strange places, sir,' I said. 'Can I tell you about it in the house?'

'Yes,' he said. 'Come in.'

We went into the house, and into a room with many books and papers. Mr Rankeillor asked me a lot of questions.

'Where were you born . . . ? Who was your father . . . ? Who was your mother . . . ? Do you have any uncles . . . ?'

After a time, he took a small book out of a cupboard and looked at it. 'Did you know a man with the name of Hoseason?' he asked.

'He kidnapped me,' I said. And I told him about it. He listened carefully. 'The ship went on the rocks.'

'Where?' he asked.

'South of the island of Mull,' I said.

'Yes,' Mr Rankeillor said. 'But the ship went down . . . ' (he looked at his notebook) '. . . on 27th June. We are now in August. Your friends are not very happy. What can you tell me about those two months?'

'I can tell you everything,' I said. 'But am I talking to a friend?'

He smiled. 'You are thinking, "This man was my uncle's lawyer." But "was" is the right word. Your friend Mr Campbell was here, and I learned many things about Mr Ebenezer Balfour. I do not work for him now.'

'Sir,' I said, 'I will put a friend's life into your hands when I tell you my story.'

'It will be all right,' he said. 'But we will call your friend "Mr Thomson", please. I can't remember Highland names.'

I told him my story.

At the end of it, he said, 'Your friend Mr Thomson is a very interesting man. But perhaps a difficult man. Our lives will be easier when he leaves us. For Holland, perhaps. Now I have to think. You can wash, and then I'll find some of my son's clothes for you.'

He gave me a wonderful lunch. It was my first good food for many weeks. And he told me the story of my father and my uncle.

'Ebenezer was the younger brother,' he said. 'He was a beautiful boy. His mother and father gave him everything and did everything for him. Your father helped him too. When the two boys fell in love with the same girl, Ebenezer thought, "She'll want to marry me."

'But your mother, David, did not want Ebenezer. He was very angry. He did and said bad things. Your grandmother and grandfather were very sad, and later ill. Then they died. Your father was a kind man, but he was weak. In the end, he and the girl went away. They left the house of Shaws to the bad younger brother.'

Chapter 14   Shaws Again

'Hoseason kidnapped you because your uncle asked him,' said Rankeillor. 'We have to hear him say that. Then we do not have to use the law. We can take the house and the other things. They are yours. And we won't have to ask Mr Thomson for his story.'

Mr Rankeillor called the man in the next office. The man worked for Mr Rankeillor. Then we went to Shaws. On the way, I ran into the trees and told Alan our plan. He laughed and came with me.

'Mr Thomson, this is nice,' said Rankeillor. 'But I forgot my glasses, so I won't know you again. Perhaps we won't meet again. I know a ship's captain, and he'll take you to Holland tomorrow.'

It was dark when we came to the house of Shaws. We looked, but we could see no lights anywhere in the house.

'My uncle is in bed,' I said quietly.

Mr Rankeillor and his man and I went across to the house and stood near the wall. Alan waited, then he went to the front door. He hit it hard.

After some minutes, I heard a noise. Ebenezer opened a window. He had his gun.

'Who is it?' he called down. 'I have my gun! And I'll shoot!'

But Alan was not afraid of the gun. 'Is that you, Mr Balfour?'

he shouted. Then he smiled. 'Be careful with that gun. They are dangerous things.'

'What do you want?' called Ebenezer. 'Who are you?'

'I'm here about David,' shouted Alan.

'Be quiet!' said Ebenezer. 'Don't shout. Which David are you talking about?'

Alan stopped shouting, but he said, loudly, 'David Balfour. Now come down, and we will talk.'

Ebenezer came down slowly and opened the front door of the house. Then he spoke.

'Yes?' he said.

'David Balfour,' Alan said again. 'We've got him. Now, do you like the boy? You can pay us and we'll bring him home again. Or don't you want him? You can pay us and we'll lose him for you. What do you think?'

My uncle did not speak.

'Answer, before I take my sword to you!' shouted Alan.

'Wh-what!' said my uncle. 'What's wrong with you? I'm trying to think.'

'Then try quickly!' said Alan.

'What do you want me to pay?' my uncle asked.

'What did you pay Hoseason?' asked Alan.

'What do you mean?' said Ebenezer.

'When he kidnapped David,' said Alan.

'How do you know about Hoseason?' said my uncle.

'I work with Hoseason,' said Alan. 'We're friends. You'll pay us a hundred pounds and we'll lose the boy for you. Is that right?'

'No, that's not right!' said Ebenezer. 'I only gave Hoseason twenty pounds. Not a penny more. He can get more when he sells the boy in the Carolinas, but not a penny more from me. No. I can't give him more than twenty pounds.'

'Thank you, Mr Balfour,' said Rankeillor. He moved away from the wall, and now Ebeneezer could see him.

My uncle looked at me, and his eyes opened wide.

'What– !' began my uncle.

'We know everything now,' said Rankeillor. 'I have some papers here. You will put your name to them. My man will put his name to them too because he heard everything.'

Rankeillor's man moved away from the wall.

'And Mr David Balfour is here too,' Rankeillor told my uncle.

I came out from my place by the wall of the house.

My uncle could not speak. He looked at me, and his eyes opened wide. Some minutes later, Mr Rankeillor had to help him into the kitchen. We followed them and Mr Rankeillor put the old man down on a chair.

'Now, Mr Ebenezer,' said Rankeillor. 'We will not be difficult. Give us the key to your wine cupboard and we'll get a bottle of wine. This is a happy day.'

Now Mr Rankeillor turned to me.

'Mr David,' he said. 'I hope you will be happy here, in your house. In *your* house.'

'In *my* house,' I said happily.

ACTIVITIES

Chapters 1–4

Before you read

1 Work with another student.

   a Look at the map and the other pictures in the book. Does this story happen in Britain? When?

   b Read the Introduction. Were you right?

2 Look at the Word List at the back of the book. Find new words in your dictionary.

   a Six of these words are for people. Which words?

   b Which of these things can you see on a good map?

While you read

3 Finish each sentence with one word.

   a Mr Campbell gives David a ....

   b David has to take the letter to the house of ....

   c David's father was a ....

   d The only .... in the house comes from the fire.

   e Mr Ebenezer Balfour comes to the window with a ....

4 Which are the right words?

   a David's father was Ebenezer Balfour's *uncle / brother*.

   b There are no *lights / fires* in any rooms in the house of Shaws.

   c Ebenezer was *younger / older* than David's father.

   d When David goes up the outside stairs, he carries a *light / key*.

   e David thinks that Mr Balfour wants to *help / murder* him.

5 What happens first? Number the sentences, 1–6.

   a David and his uncle go onto the ship.   4

   b Somebody hits David on the head.   5

   c A boy brings a letter for Mr Balfour.   1

   d David's uncle leaves on the ship's boat.   6

   e David and his uncle arrive at the Hawes Hotel.   3

   f The boy tells David about the *Covenant*.   2

38

6 What are the names of these people in the story? Write the numbers in the boxes on the left.

a David's uncle	3	1	Rankeillor
b the lawyer	.....	2	Riach
c the captain of the *Covenant*	.....	3	Ebenezer Balfour
d the first officer	.....	4	Hoseason
e the second officer	.....	5	Ransome
f the ship's boy	.....	6	Shuan

After you read

7 Why are these things important in the story?

    a a letter from David's father

    b lightning

8 Answer these questions.

    a On the first night Ebenezer Balfour turns the key in David's door. On the second night David turns the key in his uncle's door. Why do they do this?

    b What happens to Ransome?

9 Work with another student. Have this conversation.

    Student A: You are David. You are walking near Cramond, to the house of Shaws. You meet a man on the road and ask him the way. Ask him about the house and the people in it.

    Student B: You meet a young man on the road near Cramond. Answer his questions.

Chapters 5–9

Before you read

10 David is on the ship. Ransome is dead and David has to take his place. What will happen next? Which men on the ship are dangerous and which are kind? Can David get away from the ship? Discuss these questions.

11 Are these sentences right (✓) or wrong (✗)?

    a Shuan is a dangerous man when he drinks.   .....

    b When the *Covenant* hits another boat, everybody
       on it dies.   .....

    c The strange man wants to go to France.   .....

    d He gives the captain sixty pounds   .....

    e The officers want to kill the strange man.   .....

    f The man's name is really Alan Breck.   .....

12 Make three sentences about the fight in the roundhouse.

Alan Breck	kills one of the seamen	with a sword.
David	kills Mr Shuan	with a gun.
	shoots one of the seamen in the leg	

13 Finish the sentences with names from the story.

    a Alan hates all people with the name ....

    b .... is the chieftain of Alan's clan.

    c The King of England's name is ....

    d People call Colin of Glenure the ....

    e The ship hits the rocks near the island of ....

14 Which are the right words?

    a The man on Mull speaks English *well / badly*.

    b The man and his wife gives David food and drink and he gives
       them *nothing / money*.

    c When David shows Neil Roy the button, Neil Roy is suddenly
       friendly / unfriendly.

    d Neil Roy says that the red soldiers are *dangerous / friendly*.

After you read

15 Why are these words important in the story? Who says them?
Who does he say them to?

    a 'Are you one of us?'

    b 'He can get the guns.'

    c 'Show the button anywhere.'

    d 'So, David, I carry that money.'

16 Answer these questions.

    a Why do the ship's officers send David into the roundhouse?

    b Why does Alan Breck give David a button from his coat?

    c Why will the captain take Alan to Linnhe Loch?

    d Why do the Stewarts hate the Campbells?

    e Why can't the people in the Highlands wear their Highland clothes?

Chapters 10–14

Before you read

17 David is now in the Highlands. What can he do? Where can he go? Can he go back to his uncle at the house of Shaws? Will he meet Alan Breck again? How will the story end? Discuss these questions.

While you read

18 When do these things happen in the story? Number the sentences, 1–6.

    a David meets Alan Breck again. .....

    b David sees the murderer and follows him. .....

    c The soldiers want to catch David. .....

    d Somebody kills Colin of Glenure. .....

    e David meets two men on the road. .....

    f David and Alan run for their lives. .....

19 Are these sentences right (✓) or wrong (✗)?

    a Alan Breck kills the Red Fox. .....

    b David wants to go to Stirling. .....

    c The Red Fox was a Campbell. .....

    d James Stewart does not know about Red Fox's murder. .....

    e James Stewart takes money from Alan. .....

    f Alan and David are cold and hungry when they leave James Stewart's house. .....

    g When night comes, they sleep under a rock. .....

20 Which are the right words?

    a The soldiers are watching the *rocks / river*.

    b The weather that day is *hot / wet*.

    c After four days they are very *hungry / tired*.

    d They go across the River Forth *by the bridge / in a boat*.

21 Who:

    a does not work for Ebenezer Balfour now? ....

    b is 'Mr Thomson'? ....

    c is 'the younger brother'? ....

    d asks for money from Ebenezer Balfour? ....

    e will live in the house of Shaws? ....

After you read

22 Why are these people important to the story?

    a David's friend, Mr Campbell

    b the girl in the bread shop

    c the man in the next office to Mr Rankeillor's

23 Discuss these question. What do you think? At the end of the story,

    a how does David feel about his uncle Ebenezer?

    b will David see Alan Breck again?

    c will Mr Rankeillor work for David?

24 Work with another student. Have this conversation.

    Student A: You are David Balfour. Alan Breck is going to go to Holland today. You want to say thank you for his help.

    Student B: You are Alan Breck. You are leaving today. Say thank you to David for his help in the roundhouse.

25 Answer these questions.

    a Why did David's father leave the house of Shaws to his younger brother?

    b Why did Ebenezer Balfour pay twenty pounds to Hoseason?

    c Why can David live in the house of Shaws now?

Writing

26 You are David. It is two years after the end of the story. You are living in the house of Shaws now. The house is very different. Where is your uncle living? Write a letter to Alan Breck.

27 Which person in the story is the most interesting to you? Why? Write about him or her.

28 Ebenezer Balfour is a strange man. He was a beautiful boy and his father and mother gave him everything. Later he was a bad and dangerous man in a dark house. What happened? Write about him.

29 You are Mr Rankeillor. You find the address of the family of Ransome, the ship's boy. They want to know about his life on the ship. What happened to him? Write a letter to his parents and tell them.

30 You are the girl in the bread shop in Stirling. Every day you write about your life and work in a little book. One day two strange men came into your shop. What happened that day? Write about it.

31 Captain Hoseason kidnapped David and took him onto his ship. David was afraid. Was there a time when you were in a dangerous place? When? Where? Why? What happened? Write the story.

32 What did you learn from this story about Scotland and its people at this time? Write about them.

33 Did you enjoy *Kidnapped*? What did you like? What did you not like? Write about it for your friends.

Answers for the Activities in this book are available from the Penguin Readers website. A free Activity Worksheet is also available from the website. Activity Worksheets are part of the Penguin Teacher Support Programme, which also includes Progress Tests and Graded Reader Guidelines. For more information, please visit:
www.penguinreaders.com.

WORD LIST *with example sentences*

button (n) I lost a *button* from my coat.

captain (n) The *captain* took the ship south to Argentina.

chieftain (n) The *chieftain* called his people to a meeting.

clan (n) Most people in these villages are from the same *clan*.

fox (n) A *fox* came in the night and ate the chickens.

hill (n) Let's climb the *hill* and have lunch on the top.

island (n) You can take a boat from here to the *islands*.

key (n) Can I have the *key* to the front door? I can't get into the house.

kidnap (v/adj) Two men *kidnapped* my wife and I had to pay them a lot of money. After ten days, I found my *kidnapped* children.

king (n) Please stand up before the *king* comes into the room.

land (n) After three hours on the boat, she wanted to be on *land* again.

law (n) The *law* says that you cannot kill.

She is going to see a *lawyer* because her husband left her last week.

lightning (n) *Lightning* killed him when he got out of the car.

murder (n/v) The police are asking questions about the *murder* of a child in a house in this street.

officer (n) The men drank all night because the ship's *officers* were asleep.

rock (n) Leave your money under a *rock*, and let's swim in the sea.

roundhouse (n) The *roundhouse* is the best room on the ship.

shoot (v) Don't *shoot*! Put the gun down!

soldier (n) He was a *soldier* for years, but he never fought.

sword (n) They fought with *swords*, and the loser died.